Walking Silverton

HISTORY, SIGHTS, *and* STORIES

Beverly Rich

with photographs by
Casey Carroll

San Juan County Historical Society
PO Box 154, Courthouse Square
Silverton, Colorado 81433

Copyright © 2014 **Ballantine Communications, Inc.**

All rights reserved, including the right to reproduce this book or portions thereof in any form, store in a retrieval system, or transmit in any form or by any means, electronic, mechanical, photocopy, recording, or otherwise without permission in writing from the publisher, except by a reviewer who may quote brief passages in a review.

Beverly Rich

with photographs by
Casey Carroll

ISBN: 979-8-218-00737-9

Editor: Elizabeth A. Green
Design and Layout: Lisa Snider

www.sanjuancountyhistoricalsociety.org

Get Ready,

For such a small town, there's a lot to see in Silverton. This book will help you explore our town and learn a bit about the people, places, and events that are part of our rich history.

Think of this tour as a scavenger hunt through time and events. At designated stops, you'll have a clue photo to guide you to interesting buildings and landmarks. Turn the page, and you'll find a collection of photos and stories that will enlighten, amuse, and inform you.

Who knew history could be so much fun?

Your tour starts at the courthouse, toward the north end of Greene Street. You will walk through a residential area, past churches and other important places, and on to our main commercial street. Then you'll stroll along notorious Blair Street before returning to the courthouse.

FYI:
Silverton's main streets were laid out parallel to the river. To simplify things, we'll say named streets run north-south, while numbered streets run east-west.

The map on the back cover will keep you on track. Since street signs are rare in Silverton, directions are given by blocks and turns. Greene is the only paved street in town, and some of our sidewalks are historic features themselves. Watch your footing, and remember that cars use the streets as well as pedestrians.

The houses on this tour are privately owned, so please view them from the street or sidewalk.

The full tour is two miles long, and most people complete it in one and a half to two hours. It easily can be divided into segments to accommodate time restrictions or interests.

Be aware of the elevation – 9,300 feet – and stop to rest if necessary.

Have fun! Take your camera! Stop for water or refreshments along the way.

Note to Train Passengers:
You can tour at least Greene and Blair streets by starting the tour at any of the restaurants along those streets. Just ask the server where you are on the map, and let them know you're taking the tour and don't want to linger over your meal.

KEY:

 You found it!

Boldface type in the text will identify individuals in photographs.

As you walk the streets of Silverton, you will be struck by the degree to which time has stood still here. This town's past is in evidence everywhere you look.

This place is a historic treasure – to such a degree that the town in its entirety was designated as a National Historic Landmark District on July 4, 1961. To qualify for this distinction, a town (or district) must contain buildings, structures, sites, or objects that have national-level historical significance. That means that while not every building is historically significant, the majority of them are.

When the National Register of Historic Places was established in 1966, Silverton was automatically included. Of the 85,000 places on the register, only about 2,500 are National Historic Landmarks.

This is a very special place.

Get Set,

Utes had lived and hunted in this valley for centuries before gold was discovered in the early 1860s. Soon after that discovery, the San Juans were crawling with prospectors, who named the valley Baker's Park. The government forced the Utes out in 1874, opening the San Juans to settlement. Silverton's early residents were from the eastern United States but soon immigrants from all over the world arrived. The earliest structures were canvas tents and log cabins, or a combination of the two.

The main route into Silverton was a wagon road over Stony Pass from Salida. To say that it was passable by wagon was stretching the truth – many times wagons had to be moved with block and tackle cinched to trees. Getting the ore out of the San Juans and supplies into the mining camps was expensive and difficult. With the arrival of the Denver & Rio Grande Railroad in 1882, ore was more easily exported, and supplies were easier to obtain.

Silverton became the center of commerce for the San Juan mining region and, with its four railroads and three smelters, served gold and silver mines with names like the Sunnyside, the Gold King, and the Old Hundred high up in the mountains – many of them financed by eastern investors who never set foot in the San Juans. Men worked and lived in boarding houses at these remote locations year-round. They came into town in ore buckets over long cable tram lines extending from the mines down into the canyons. Many of the miners spent their money in Blair Street's saloons and houses of ill repute.

By 1910 San Juan County had its highest population: 5,000 residents, including many inventive, hard-working, resourceful people. Silverton was at its apex of wealth, a symbol of the great industrial revolution equipped with electric lights, telephones, and businesses that could provide everything people needed, from fine clothing to a new wagon and locally brewed beer.

In the years since, boom and bust cycles typical of the mining industry have made fortunes and then sent them plummeting. Boom times have brought influxes of peoples from every ethnic group on earth, and the bust times have turned communities into ghostly reminders of themselves.

Today Silverton is the only town left in the county, with a population of 600, supported by tourists who come to see the magnificent scenery and experience the remarkable history of the area.

... Go!

Start in the museum parking lot and look for this rooster on top of a cupola.

 You have found the San Juan County Courthouse.

San Juan County Courthouse

With its imposing size and location the stately **courthouse** is the cornerstone of the Silverton National Historic Landmark District, built for $79,000 in 1907. Starting in 1876, San Juan County's offices led a gypsy-like existence around Silverton, including leased space on the second floor of the Grand Hotel. When Colorado law required every county to have a courthouse thirty years later, the county commissioners established a two-year tax levy to finance it. By the time the courthouse opened, it was fully paid for.

It is built of golden/gray brick with white sandstone trimmings and an ornate clock tower dome gilded in gold leaf. Pennsylvania black slate covers the roof. Inside, the county offices have original furnishings, brass chandeliers, and tiled floors. Up the sweeping staircase, arranged around the cupola, are the elegant courtrooms and judge's chambers, with glass-fronted bookcases and maple floors.

IMAGINE THIS

Look to the right of the courthouse and imagine burly miners seeing this imposing three-story building on the horizon when they arrived in Silverton in 1903. As they made their way to notorious Blair Street, ready to join in the reverie, the new state-of-the-art San Juan County Jail stood as an imposing reminder that they should toe the line, or else.

A LADY WITH TRUE GRIT
Alice Hendrickson Kimball

was the first woman county assessor in America. Born in 1877 near the site of present-day Electra Lake, she was the first teacher at the school in Howardsville. She married Orlo D. Kimball, an early day mine owner, and the couple had two sons.

Alice gained deep knowledge of the mining industry from Orlo. When he died in 1917 she was well-prepared to be county assessor. She held the elective office from 1918 to 1937.

Alice showed true pioneer grit. In 1932, when snow blocked the railroad and roads, county assessors were meeting in Durango. The closest the train could get to Silverton was Needleton. Alice, who was 55, rode horseback four-

teen miles down the Animas canyon through deep snow and over snowslides, boarded the train and attended the meeting.

During the 1932 blockade, the train could not bring supplies, passengers, mail, or parcel post to Silverton for ninety days.

Remember, named streets run north-south. Walk south to the corner and turn right. Walk one block, looking for this house detail ahead as you go, then stop at the corner.

 This Queen Anne house is on Reese Street.

REESE STREET

This neighborhood is an example of Victorian era architecture, a term that refers to styles popularized during the reign of Queen Victoria, 1837-1901. Most houses in Silverton were built between 1880 and 1910.

Queen Anne style is the most common Victorian era style in Silverton, with steeply pitched roofs that can shed heavy winter snow. The style also includes a front-facing gable with patterned shingles; porches with delicate spindle columns; and lacy brackets at porch corners. These features are called "gingerbread."

Reese Street was named after Dempsey Reese, one of a group of miners who signed a pledge to donate some of their ore to whoever would build a working smelter in Baker's Park. The new town soon had three smelters, including the Greene Smelter on the flanks of Boulder Mountain to the north of this neighborhood. Reese held numerous civic offices, and the first hook and ladder fire department was named after him.

PROSPERITY

Mines, mills, and smelters were the core of Silverton's economy. Mines yielded ore that contained lead, zinc, copper, silver, and – most coveted of all – gold. Long aerial tramlines carried rock from the mines to the mills, which ground it to a powder and separated out the concentrates. Smelters then refined the concentrates to pure metals. Silverton's big coal-burning smelters filled the valley with black smoke – this was the smell, sound, and look of prosperity. Before long, though, they were replaced by more efficient smelters at lower elevation.

The **Kendrick-Gelder Smelter** was built in 1900 at the base of Boulder Mountain. It specialized in treating ores rich in pyrite and copper from the Great Gold King Mine, which were brought to the smelter by the Silverton Gladstone and Northerly Railroad. The smelter closed in 1908.

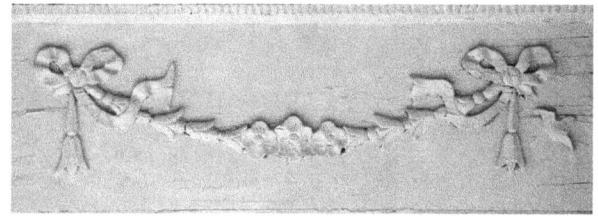

Turn left (this is Reese Street) and walk one-half block.
Look to your left and find this front door decoration.

WALKING SILVERTON

GREENE & CO. HOUSE

Ben Harwood and Edward Greene built this house – Silverton's oldest – in 1874, to house three families associated with Greene & Co. mercantile, which was across the street. The Greene and William Earl families lived upstairs and the Harwoods lived downstairs. In his prime, Ben Harwood was the most powerful, untiring man in the district. For several winters he packed the mail on snowshoes over Stony Pass to Howardsville, while at the same time carrying 50-80 pounds of beef on his back to be dropped off at the Highland Mary Mine, and other mine supplies. He first worked in the area as a freighter, and packed in all the building materials for the Greene Smelter, the first in the San Juans. He then branched out into building roads through solid rock up to 14 feet deep. His capacity for work was amazing.

You found it – Silverton's oldest surviving home.

OLDEST HOME

Silverton's first white baby was born in this house in July 1875, to Byron and Sarah Taft. Lacking any other available fabrics, Sarah crafted baby Anna's clothing from red flannel underwear and heavy blue shirts. The infant was welcomed by the Silverton band, and local merchants offered an array of gifts to celebrate her arrival. Anna's middle name honored her birthplace: Silverton.

SUNNY SOLSTICE

For a period of time around the winter solstice the sun comes up twice in Silverton. It comes up on the north side of **Kendall Peak** first, travels behind the peak, then rises again on the south side.

Walk one-half block to the intersection and cross the street, then find this sign on a house at the corner.

 The Cotton House was the social center of early Silverton.

THE COTTONS

John and **Amanda Cotton**'s home was the social center of town, where friends gathered to play cards, tell fortunes, or swap reminiscences. The Cottons often provided music – John on violin and Amanda on melodeon – for dances, one of the few forms of recreation in Silverton. The couple arrived among the earliest settlers in 1874. As one of the few white women in a community of prospectors and miners, Amanda overcame unbelievable hardships with good cheer and common sense. She accumulated a great deal of mining property and real estate, and operated hotels, boarding houses, and a vegetable store. Amanda won an award at the 1893 Chicago World's Fair for her outstanding display of minerals. She was known as a friend to people of all ages, classes, and conditions.

IN THE HEART OF MOUNTAINS

Kendall Mountain on the west side of Silverton is named after James W. Kendall, a prospector who arrived in the district in 1872. Kendall concentrated his prospecting activities on this imposing, 13,066-foot alp. To the north of Silverton is **Boulder Mountain,** a name which has yet to win recognition on a government map. It is 13,248 feet at its summit and traditionally has been considered part of 13,487-foot Storm Peak right behind it. The peaks to the south are Sultan Mountain at 13,368 feet and Grand Turk at 13,087 feet. Local lore holds that the latter resembles a turbaned head from certain vantage points.

To the north is Anvil Mountain, a relatively barren peak bearing definite signs of its volcanic origins. The earliest prospectors called it Indian Head.

Continue for one block and stop at the corner.
Can you find this light/sign across the intersection?

MEN'S MEETINGS

In 1893 the **Masonic Lodge**, which was chartered in 1878, purchased this building after fire destroyed their original meeting space and records. The second floor was leased to the Silverton Men's Club. In 1902 the Masons extended the building to the alley, and built a beautiful lodge room on the second floor and apartments underneath.

 You have found the Masonic Hall.

Through the years the lodge fostered community involvement, advanced the welfare of the town's citizens and sponsored social functions for all ages.

PAPER HISTORY

Before the Masons, two of the earliest newspapers in the San Juans were housed in this 1883 building. Newspaper pioneer John R. Curry hauled an 1839 press over the mountains by pack train to begin publishing the *La Plata Miner* in July 1875. When snowstorms and slides cut off the town for several weeks, he had the newspaper printed on butcher's wrapping paper. It merged with the *Silverton Standard* (founded in 1889) 1922, creating the *Silverton Standard and Miner*, the oldest continuously operating newspaper and business on the Western Slope. The Society of Professional Journalists designated it a National Historic Site in Journalism.

MEN'S CLUBS

Silverton has had numerous fraternal organizations, including Masons, Odd Fellows, Knights of Pythias, Elks, Eagles, and **Woodmen of the World** (which also provided burial insurance). These social and philanthropic clubs signified civilization in frontier towns like Silverton, promoting personal development, extending aid to those in need, combatting vice in every form, and serving as great moral influences. Many had fenced burial plots at the cemetery for their members.

Turn right and walk one block west.
Cross the street and look for this cornerstone.

 You can still see a doctor or nurse in this former hospital.

NOT JUST FOR MINERS

The **Miners' Union Hospital**, designed by F. E. Edbrooke (Tabor Opera House, State Capitol) was built in 1907 when union membership was at its peak. The Italianate style exemplified the union's strength and influence. The basement had doctor quarters; the first floor, wards; and the third floor, private rooms, doctor offices, and the operating room, with large solarium windows.

The county-owned building remains the town's only health care facility, with a county nurse and a visiting doctor. It also houses other offices and services, including the newspaper and food pantry.

ON THIS SPOT

Capt. Charles Baker discovered gold when in this valley, which was initially named in his honor. After the Civil War (1861-1865), prospectors arrived in large numbers and Silverton was incorporated in 1874.

What is believed to have been the first building in the town of Silverton stood on this site. The **log cabin** was built in 1874 by Francis M. Snowden, an early prospector in the San Juans and was a gathering spot in the town's early years.

DANGERS OF MINING

Mining was extremely dangerous, with blasting, open shafts, and cave-ins causing frequent, often fatal accidents. The luckier **miners** were only blinded, maimed, or crippled for life. Safety was of little concern, since many mine owners considered mules more valuable than men. The high altitude, up to 14,000 feet, guaranteed a harsh environment and long, freezing winters with numerous deadly snowslides. The supply of alcohol was abundant and saloons, gambling, and prostitution contributed to many violent deaths as well.

Turn left (Snowden Street), walk one block south and cross the street. See if you can find this school bell.

You can blame the Romans for the apparent typo in PVBLIC.

SILVERTON SCHOOL

This 1911 brick structure replaced a two-story wooden building that was deemed a fire hazard. The depression era Works Progress Administration built the gym in the 1930s. About 80 children currently attend kindergarten through 12th grade, using the innovative Expeditionary Learning curriculum, which encourages respect, responsibility, integrity, compassion, courage, and involvement in the community. In 2010 a major grant financed restoration of the school and gym. San Juan County taxpayers passed a bond issue providing matching funds. The restoration included updating the mechanical systems, adding a cafeteria, and installing high-tech upgrades. The school became the first in Colorado to be certified LEED (Leadership in Energy and Environmental Design) Gold, for its energy efficiency and "green" construction.

The school is the center of community activity in Silverton, hosting sports events, theater productions, reunions, and more. Every year the Catholics host the community Thanksgiving dinner in the performing arts center and a month later the Protestants host the annual Christmas dinner here.

"PVBLIC" is American Classical architecture's nod to the Romans, and is commonly found on libraries and schools built between the late 1800s and mid-1900s.

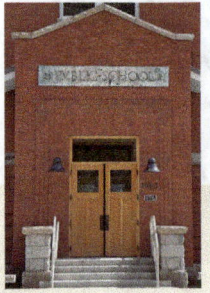 

RUNNING RUGGED

Runners in the **HARDROCK 100** pass through some of the most beautiful and rugged mountains in the world, linking the mountain towns Lake City, Ouray, Telluride, and Silverton. They start and finish at the Silverton School, and must complete the 100-mile course within 48 hours. Using established trails as much as possible and running through the night, they reach an average elevation of about 11,000 feet, with a high point of 14,048 feet on Handies Peak.

8

Walk to the end of the block and look up to your right.
Do you see this cross?

WALKING SILVERTON

 Several denominations have called this church home.

CHURCH ON THE HILL

This church was erected in 1898 as St. John's Episcopal Church. A shortage of funds resulted in it being rented to the school for overflow classrooms until 1901, when it was furnished and opened as a church. The belfry came from the old school at the ghost town of Eureka.

The funeral for Otto Mears, known as the Pathfinder of the San Juans, was held in this church after he died in California at the age of 90, in 1931. The man who was largely responsible for transportation development in Western Colorado had asked that his ashes and those of his wife and daughter be scattered in his beloved San Juan Mountains.

This building has subsequently housed the Foursquare Church and now, the Southern Baptists.

A PATHFINDER
Otto Mears
was born to English and Russian parents in 1840, and orphaned at a young age. He was passed from relative to relative until he ended up alone in California at the age of 11. He found jobs, learned English, and volunteered for the Civil War. He found his way to Santa Fe after the war, and eventually to Colorado, first as a merchant and then as a packer. Mears helped negotiate with Ute Chief Ouray when the San Juans were opened to mining, and built toll roads and railroads that helped open up mining districts in the region. Mears became a wealthy man and dabbled in politics before retiring to California.

24

This one's hard. Continue straight to the middle of the block and look up to your right to find this Victorian era gingerbread.

| 25

 A Russian immigrant designed this house.

FIT FOR A PRINCESS

Emma Harris was born in Odessa, Russia, the daughter of Baronet Von Lassberg Blumenstock, a general in the Russian army. She came to America in 1866, and in 1881, she and her husband, William D. Harris, a miner, came to Silverton. Emma planned and decorated this beautiful residence in 1886. It was built by her very good friend, F. O. Sherwood. In partnership with Sherwood, she designed three more houses in Silverton, all architecturally notable for their flamboyant detailing and gingerbread. A devout spiritualist, she died at the age of 43, with her husband her only heir. Her **grave** at Hillside Cemetery is distinctive with its stonework base, red brick cupola, and now broken glassed-in alcove, where legend says that her jewels were displayed.

QUALITY HILL

Snowden Street was named for **Francis Marion Snowden**, whose log cabin was the first in Baker's Park. One of the original platters of the town site, Snowden lived in Silverton until he was an old man and was both marshal and mayor at various times. Some of Silverton's most influential residents lived on this street, which some called "Quality Hill."

Turn around and go back one-half block, then turn right (11th Street). Walk one block and look for a brick building. Can you see this keystone arch?

 There's that PVBLIC again, on the Silverton Library.

FOR ALL READERS

The **Silverton Library** is a special gem in this architecturally rich town. It retains its original furnishings and lamps, with a children's section and a reading room in the basement. As in all modern libraries, it offers computer and internet service. The library was built in 1906 for $12,000, financed by philanthropist Andrew Carnegie, who made his fortune in steel. A total of 1,689 Carnegie libraries were built in the U.S. between 1883 and 1929, nearly half of all the libraries in America. Library hours are posted on the front door and visitors are welcome to explore inside.

CARNEGIE LIBRARIES

There were 35 Carnegie libraries built in Colorado, but only three on the Western Slope. Five have been demolished and many others now house private businesses, residences, or government offices. Carnegie grants in Colorado ranged from $6,500 to $70,000 for individual libraries. Denver received $350,000 to build nine libraries.

> 👉 **Turn and look at the church across the intersection.**

A PASTOR

Like most small town pastors, Rev. Marvin Hudson served more than one church. He also taught sixth grade at the local school. Rev. Hudson was on his way from Ouray to the Silverton Congregational Church in March 1963, when his car got stuck coming through the canyon. He had stopped to put on chains when the notorious East Riverside Slide ran. It swept the car, with Hudson and his daughters Amelia and Pauline, over the cliff, killing all three. Pauline's body wasn't found until spring. The slide has run so often that its path is almost devoid of vegetation.

FIRST CHURCH

Silverton's Congregational Church is the seventh oldest in Colorado and the oldest on the Western Slope. The church was organized in 1878 and the building constructed in 1881, except for the steeple, which was added in 1892. The parsonage next door was built in 1884. According to paint samples taken during a major restoration several years ago, the original color of the church was red! When asked if they wanted the church restored to its original color, the congregation adamantly said "NO."

Now turn right (on Reese) and walk one block.
Look to your right to find this copper cross on a door.

WALKING SILVERTON

 This is one of five churches in Silverton.

BUILT BY MINERS

St. Patrick's Catholic Church was built in 1905, at a cost of about $9,000 and the parish house next door in 1906. Much of the masonry was done by Italian miners as volunteers. The original wooden church was given to the black population, which numbered about 50 at that time. They came to Silverton to take the service jobs that were opened by the removal of the Chinese population in 1902. They moved the old church down the hill to Mineral Street, where it was used as a house of worship for the newly organized African Methodist Episcopal congregation. The Catholic Church has undergone renovation in recent years, including re-installation of a stained glass window in the back wall of the church. It had been removed years ago.

THE MEARS HOME

Only the upstairs front windows are unchanged on the house across the street, where **Otto Mears** lived for many years. From 1889 to 1892 Mears issued complimentary **railroad passes** to his partners, special friends, and biggest customers. These were no ordinary passes – they were made out of silver! One year it was a silver watch fob, the next a solid silver pass, and the next a silver filigree pass. To the most special people (including his wife Mary), he gave the rarest of all – a buckskin pass.

Turn left and walk one block to Greene Street.
Cross the street and and find this
beautiful window on the front of the corner house.

VICTORIAN GEM

This Queen Anne style house with the ornate gingerbread and lovely stained glass was the third house built by Emma Harris, the Russian princess. She sold her big house on Quality Hill to Mayor J. W. Wingate in 1890 and moved to this house. She passed away in 1895 and "her spirit took flight to that shore where time is not and delights bloom to wither never."

 This house was also designed by the Russian princess.

☞ **Now turn around, and look to the west. Look for Christ of the Mines Shrine on Anvil Mountain.**

DOWN TIMES

In the 1950s there were no more working mines in the San Juans. The Catholic Men's Club decided a shrine dedicated to miners might help. The statue of Christ was made of Carrara marble from Italy, Mother Country for many Silverton miners. After the shrine's completion, the American Tunnel was built under old Sunnyside Mine workings, and mining became profitable again.

WATER HAVOC

On June 4, 1978, Lake Emma broke through the Sunnyside Mine from high above it, flooding the underground workings and destroying everything in its path before it gushed out the lower portal. Yet a miracle had occurred. The mine flooded on a Sunday night, when no men were working. The flood shut down the mine for a while, but did not claim a single life.

Stay on the same side of Greene Street and walk one and a half blocks north. Stop and look for these arched windows across the street.

 You have found what was originally the Past Time Saloon.

TO MARKET

This was the **Silverton Meat and Produce** company, built by pioneer butcher Fred Hemboldt in 1893. Cattle and hogs were shipped by train in stock cars to Hemboldt's stockyard near the depot. Several lodges used the upstairs, including the Woodsmen of the World, who later purchased the building. It became the San Juan Bar in 1933 and has been a bar and restaurant since then.

Silverton also had a fish farm. Fish were stocked in a pond just north of the town limits, were harvested all summer, and salted or smoked to store them for the winter. There also were two dairies that furnished milk, cream, and butter to Silverton residents and to the high mountain boarding houses at the mines. San Juan County has a very short growing season, so almost all of the produce for people, and hay for cattle, horses, and mules, was brought up on the train.

BY DESIGN

Silverton was designed to have nine streets running parallel to the river, four of them named for the town's founders. Thoroughfares were to be 100 feet wide, crossed at regular intervals by fifteen numbered streets that were 80 feet wide. Greene Street was named after **George Greene,** who built the first smelter in Silverton in 1875 and ran the first store. When George passed away in 1880, his family went back to Iowa and by the time the train arrived in 1882, his name was history to most residents.

Continue north on this side of Greene Street to end of the block. Look across the street to find this colorful corbel.

 This decorative support bracket adorns the Grand Imperial Hotel.

NOT A HOTEL

The **Grand Hotel** was not meant to be a hotel at all. Built in 1882 by Englishman W. S. Thompson, it was intended to house four stores on the main floor, with government and private offices upstairs. But the following year, the owner turned the third story into a hotel, which he called the Grand. A local newspaper reported the arrival of the iron front for the structure, adding that the brick work was progressing rapidly. Remarkably, this large building, with everything

from excavation to carpentry done by hand, was completed in less than a year. In 1909 it was renamed the Imperial Hotel, and in 1950 became the Grand Imperial.

> **Look up the street for Fetch's Mercantile.**

THE CLUB

A Chinese laundry once stood right here. Mining entrepreneur **Thomas Blair** moved it and built this structure as a saloon in 1883. Into the 1900s the proprietors operated The Club, with liquor sales on the ground floor and various forms of gambling in both the basement and second floor. A 24-hour-a-day poker game ran here well into the 1950s, attended by some of the city's most prominent citizens.

Walk to the end of this block and stop at the corner. You'll find this spiral column on the corner building across the street.

 You have found Western Colorado's oldest commercial brick building.

RETAIL AND RECREATION

This is the **Posey & Wingate building,** built in 1880. The corner section housed the First National Bank of Silverton from 1883 to 1934, when the bank closed – after fully paying its depositors. The bank vault is still inside. The building then became a recreation hall with billiard tables in the back and a two-lane bowling alley. Many a boy in Silverton earned extra money by setting the bowling pins by hand. The other side of the building was a hardware store for many years.

GLITTERING DECADE

The decade right after the turn of the century in Silverton saw the construction of not just the courthouse and jail, but also the landmark Town Hall, which you'll see later in the tour. In that glittering decade, the Miners' Union Hospital and the jewel-box Carnegie library also were built. Water and sewer were put in, concrete sidewalks were laid and a municipally owned light plant provided electricity to the burgeoning town. Silverton was the center of commerce for the San Juan mining region and, with its four railroads and three smelters, served scores of gold and silver mines.

BANK ON IT

Silverton had four banks at the turn of the century: Silverton Industrial Bank, **First National Bank**, Bank of Silverton, and San Juan County Bank. There also was a branch of the Miners and Merchants Bank of Lake City.

16

Cross to the other side of Greene Street
and stand by the Posey & Wingate Building.
Can you see this geometric decoration across the street?

WALKING SILVERTON

EAT, DRINK, SLEEP

The very successful owner of the Silverton Brewery, Charles Fischer, built the **French Bakery** and **Teller House.** The upper story was a hotel named for Henry M. Teller, one of Colorado's first senators. Two saloons opened in this building. One was named The Frog, for the French, and the other, The Tyrol for Tyroleans. In 1916 the building was converted into a grocery and bakery, and remained so until the early 1970s.

 You have found the Teller House and French Bakery.

 Look at the adjoining building to the south.

RENT-A-HORSE

The Exchange Livery, which was built by the Doud brothers, sheltered buggies and wagons on the first floor while horses were stabled on the second floor. Miners needing a ride to a claim would rent a horse for $2, ride to their location, then let the horse loose. The horse would find its way back to town and up the ramp to its stall in the livery. The Douds were also very active in the packing industry, and later owned one of the first automobile franchises in Silverton.

OUTLAWS RUN AMOK

A gang of outlaws wrought havoc throughout Southwest Colorado in the early 1880s. When they rode into Silverton one day in August 1881, town marshal **Clayt Ogsbury** and two other men went to confront them. In front of the Diamond Saloon near this spot, a figure stepped out from the shadows and fired. Ogsbury was hit and died from his wounds. In the following days, irate townspeople took first one and then a second member of the gang from the jail and lynched them. The leaders of the gang went unpunished.

Continue south on Greene to the corner.
This sign is over a doorway on a building across the street.

The Benson Block houses Silverton's only bank.

ARCHITECTURAL SHIFT

Built only 20 years after the Grand Imperial Hotel, the **Benson Block** reflects a shift in architectural styles. While the 1882 hotel has copious embellishments and a mansard roof, the 1901 Benson Block is understated, with classical lines and less ornamentation. It was built by pioneer barkeep and miner Knute Benson, using profits from mines at Ophir. Harold "Kid" Whitelaw opened the County Club in the corner, featuring the most expensive bar fixtures ever imported to Silverton. Within a year, though, Benson was dead and Whitelaw was out of business. Over the years, the building has housed a hotel, a series of saloons, the Vienna Café, and one of the town's first automotive garages.

SHUTTERBUG

John Lorenzen and Joe Grivette wanted their **Chicago Saloon** to look elegant when they built it in 1896, so they included a distinctive bay window. Lorenzen documented the town and region

with a special camera that produced 6-by-3-inch panoramic photographs, many of which were hand-tinted. He made sure he was in every photo by setting up the camera, running to the far side, and pressing a bulb.

"STEEL-DRIVIN' MEN"

Hardrockers' Holidays have been an annual tradition in Silverton from early days. Hard-working miners show off their physical prowess in what is called double jacking. In miner's lingo, a double jack is a sledge hammer, a shovel is a muck stick and the piece of metal that they use to drill holes in rock faces underground is a hand steel. One miner holds the drill steel against the rock while his partner hits it, and turns the steel a quarter turn between blows. If a blow misses the steel, it can mangle a man's hand. The team that makes the deepest hole fastest wins, and the pair are decreed the best miners in the San Juans.

Continue south on Greene Street to the middle of the block. Look across the street for this light-festooned brick archway.

FANCIEST STABLES

The **Bowman and Melton livery stable**, built in 1897, had Silverton's first elevator, capable of lifting 1,500 pounds. Horses were kept upstairs and wagons on the main floor. People today wonder why odoriferous, noisy livery stables were built in the middle of the business districts. Trains and horses were the transportation of the time. People jumped on a train in Denver, and two days

Silverton had many livery stables in the early days.

later they were in Silverton, all by rail. They could rent a horse and sometimes a buggy, take care of business, return and pay for them, get back on the train and go home. We do the same now, only we fly and rent a car.

LIGHT ON IT

The new municipal light plant was built in 1902 for $3,000. Customers were charged by the light bulb, so each room in most homes had a single light bulb hanging from the center of the ceiling. People who wanted to show off their wealth had many light bulbs in each room. Look at buildings along Greene Street and see where light bulbs were used to outline architectural features. Silverton was rich, and people wanted to flaunt it.

BISCUIT MAKER

Before owning a livery stable, **Clint Bowman** had worked with his father in the Gold King Mine kitchen at Gladstone. The soda crackers his father made were a big hit with the miners, so Clint decided to share them with the world.

He sold the livery business in 1906 and moved to Denver, where he formed the Merchants Biscuit Company.

The business later was acquired by the United Biscuit Company, which became Keebler Company.

Continue south a half block to the corner.
Look straight ahead and up high to find this sign.

ALL FOR ONE

Members donated labor to build the **Miners' Union Hall** in 1901. Money also was withheld from their checks to help with the costs. When it was finished the imposing building became home to several labor and fraternal organizations in the community. The second floor contained a large dance floor where big community dances were held for many years. The Prosser undertaking business moved into the south storefront. The building now belongs to the Silverton Mountain Ski Area, which has offices in the south side and a gift store in front.

 You have found the Miners' Union Hall.

RESPONDING TO PANIC

Mine owners cut wages and increased work hours after the 1893 Silver Panic, prompting formation of the Silverton Miner's Union. By 1939, only the Mayflower Mine was still in operation. A strike called on July 4, 1939, had great support at first. But as it wore on, people worried that the town would go broke. A fight broke out at an Aug. 28 meeting in the union hall, and local union leaders were escorted out of town. The union was dissolved and the strike broken, but bitterness persisted for years.

A HAPPY OUTCOME

Silverton has the highest concentration per capita of pre-WWI architecture in the U.S., typified by this **tower house**. When Main Streets across the country were modernizing in the 1950s, the area's last mine, the Mayflower, shut down. Businesses couldn't afford to modernize, so much of the downtown stayed the same as when it was built.

Walk on Greene Street to the middle of the block.
Can you find these decorative shingles on a house to your right?

WALKING SILVERTON

 The Pascoe Opera House once packed 'em in where this house now stands.

GLITTERING DECADE GRANDEUR

In the middle of this once vibrant part of Silverton's business district, Dr. J. N. Pascoe opened his 500-seat Pascoe Opera House in 1905. The new building included a 21-foot-deep stage in the main-floor theater, dressing rooms in the basement, and a rooming house on the top floor. Silvertonians filled the theater opening night to watch "The Gold King," a musical comedy. The newspaper declared it a "first class playhouse," and for several years, the opera house hosted touring theater troupes, singers, musicians, lecturers, and even boxers. After Pascoe complained in 1909 that "fresh kids" were loitering outside the performance hall, the *Silverton Standard* warned that noisy youth could harm visitors' perceptions of Silverton more than all the saloons, gamblers, and prostitutes, because "the latter are made to behave themselves."

THE BAND

The tradition of brass band music here extends from the 1870s Moyle Brothers Band to the modern day **Silverton Brass Band,** which performs every summer Sunday and marches in the annual Fourth of July parade. The town also has hosted the Great Western Rocky Mountain Brass Band Festival every August for more than thirty years, bringing musicians from around the country to play free concerts of rousing brass band music in the school gym. The Silverton Brass Band plays wherever the fancy hits them: sometimes in the park, sometimes on Cinnamon Pass – you never know.

The pretty little figure is worth the search.
Turn left and cross Greene Street. Walk a block and a half,
crossing Blair Street, then look on the side of a building to your left.

WALKING SILVERTON

 This boarding house accommodated locals and visitors for many years.

ALMA HOUSE

This handsome stone building was constructed in 1902 by Bridget Hughes to take advantage of the commercial traffic brought in by the train. Before 1902, she and her husband Anthony ran a boarding house in a wood frame building here for many years. Anthony was a section foreman on the railroad, and they catered especially to the train crews. The **Alma House** was known for its fine food and hospitality. Bridget's son John and his wife May took over operating the Alma House after Bridget's death and ran it until 1950.

BY RAIL

Word of fabulous riches lured the Denver & Rio Grande Railroad to Silverton in 1882, over a 45-mile track from Durango through high mountains and deep canyons. Rails were laid only three feet apart – narrow gauge – because of the steep, curving route. Passengers and freight filled 10th Street, making it Silverton's main commercial street. Ore was transferred from **pack trains** and spur railroads here and taken to smelters in Durango. Wagons hauled goods to stores in town, and taxis later transported itinerant salesmen, vaudeville performers, and visitors to hotels and boarding houses.

PSSST, HERE'S A FUN DETOUR

From here, you can take a short side trip to see the **railroad depot**, extensive grounds, and rolling stock museum, located 2 ½ blocks east of here. You can see Otto Mears' Silverton Northern Engine House and Casey Jones, the rare railbus that ran to Eureka during the 1920s and 1930s. Also on display are the newly restored D&RGRR gondolas 871 and 1400.

22

Turn around and go back one-half block to the corner.
Can you find this sign across the street?

WALKING SILVERTON

 You have found the Avon Hotel, at the corner of 10th and Blair.

AVON HOTEL

Sherwood & Son's grocery, stove, and tinware store, built in 1904, also offered rooms upstairs for the bustling commercial street traffic between the depot and downtown. A major fire in 1938 inflicted significant damage. In the 1970s the building was a bar and restaurant, with many raucous parties harkening back to Blair Street's early days. The building is now a year-round hotel and hostel.

BOARDING HOUSE RULES

In the peak years, there were a dozen big mines and countless little workings in the mountains around Silverton. The bigger mines had **boarding houses** for the young, single men. The married men would jump on a train in Silverton and then ride a tram to go to work. There were many more men than women. Many were immigrants who left their families behind. Then, when situated well enough, they would send for wives, children, and other relatives. Some of the men were Civil War veter-ans who came West looking for a better life.

DRAFTED TO EXTRACT

Gold and silver were the main metals mined here in the early years. However, in later years, the emphasis was shifted to base metals lead, zinc, manganese, and copper for the war efforts. During World War II, the mines around Silverton were, in fact, banned from mining silver and gold. Extracting those base metals was considered strategic also, so men actually were drafted to work in the mines.

Turn right (on Blair Street), and walk to the middle of the block. You'll have to search a little to find this door embellishment.

WALKING SILVERTON

SHOTGUN HOUSE

The mining camp vernacular style of many smaller homes in Silverton, like the ones here, is based on simple prairie form. This functional and affordable design appealed to working-class people, many of them recent immigrants. The plan features a steeply pitched front gabled roof, small front porch with spindled supports, and minimal ornamentation. Most were only one room wide – or shotgun style – and built close to one another. Many have had additions built on in later years.

 You'll find several shotgun houses in this block of Blair Street.

MR. BLAIR

Blair Street was named after Thomas Blair, one of two original homesteaders in Baker's Park and a successful mine owner. He opened his Rosebud Saloon on Greene Street in 1880. The street named after him became the center of gambling and prostitution. It was so notorious that citizens on the south end of the street asked the Town Board to rename their more respectable, residential section Empire Street. To this day, half of the street is Blair and half Empire!

NOTORIOUS PAST

Blair Street was home to 32 saloons, gambling halls, and houses of ill-repute in a three-block stretch, with names like Mikado, North Pole, and Laundry (where they "cleaned you out"). Gamblers like Bat Masterson and Wyatt Earp played faro within their walls. From its earliest days, the street was infamous for its loud music and dance halls. Although illegal, gambling and prostitution were tolerated in early-day Silverton, as long as the "ladies" stayed behind an invisible line in the middle of Greene Street, separating them from the more "respectable" part of town.

By the 1940s most of the gambling was over and the ladies had moved on. The old saloons on Blair Street had a rebirth in the 1950s as movie sets where such westerns as *Run for Cover*, *Across the Wide Missouri*, **Maverick Queen,** and *True Grit* were filmed.

24

You'll find this touch of the Old West in the middle of the next block of Blair Street. Look for an old wooden door to your left.

WALKING SILVERTON

 These buildings depict the Old West for tourists.

ZANONI-PEDRONI SALOON

Across the street, the current Bent Elbow started as the Zanoni-Pedroni Saloon and was later the Monte Carlo Saloon, and then, with tourism in the '50s, the Monte Carlo Mercantile. The first Bent Elbow was next door, and was originally the Fattor Saloon, after its owner and madame, **Big Tillie Fattor.** That building burned down in 1968, along with three adjacent small cribs.

Gunfights were enacted here every day at high noon for many years. Gunslingers pretended to be shot, then fell from the balcony, promoting the town's western theme.

OLD TOWN SQUARE

After WWII, the great middle class in this country began to emerge. Roads were improved, vehicles got better, motor hotels sprang up, and people had enough income to travel. These were the days of Davy Crockett and Roy Rogers and America loved all things western. Silverton was right on board. Many buildings were brought in from the ghost town of Howardsville to make this little western scene and give tourists a sense of what life on the frontier was like.

LADIES OF THE EVENING

Blair Street had it all for men who were lonely or starved for affection. Some women worked in cribs, usually single rooms, and offered only brief episodes of companionship. Others worked for brothels – usually saloons – where liquor, gambling, and dancing were added to the "entertainment." The wealthier clientele could opt for a bordello, where discreet entertainments were offered in an opulent setting.

IN THE MOVIES

Blair Street served as the setting for many western movies during the 1950s and '60s. Every big Hollywood star filmed here, including Jimmy Stewart, Clark Gable, John Wayne, and even a young ingénue **Marilyn Monroe**, who played a dance hall girl in *Ticket to Tomahawk*. The train was the star of many movies. In fact, it was the movie industry that paid to have the train tracks extended from the depot to their present location on 12th Street.

EVOLUTION TO TOURISM

In the early 1950s, amidst a decline in the mining industry and the shipping of ore, the Denver & Rio Grande Western Railroad decided to abandon the Silverton branch. City fathers and business leaders from Durango and Silverton fought the plan and even travelled to Washington, D.C., to protest at hearings of the Public Utilities Commission.

When tourists started flocking to Durango to ride the train, the railroad realized the gold was in tourists, not freight, and the modern era of tourism was born. Businessmen in Silverton were quick to climb on the bandwagon and notorious Blair Street returned to its roots of separating people from their money, this time not in gambling halls but in shops and restaurants.

OLD WEST SMOG

Blair Street was a noisy place, with piano music from the dance halls 24 hours a day, shrieks of laughter and loud bragging by drunken men that could be heard for blocks. The clanging of slot machines and clicking of shot glasses against the bars was deafening. Wagons creaked up and down the streets, and the clopping of horse hooves was incessant. Silverton was dirty too. There were four railroads operating, with engines whistling and chugging as they spewed coal smoke up each valley. Two smelters belched smoke, one on each end of town. Adding to the foul air, Silverton burned coal in furnaces and stoves to keep houses and businesses warm in winter.

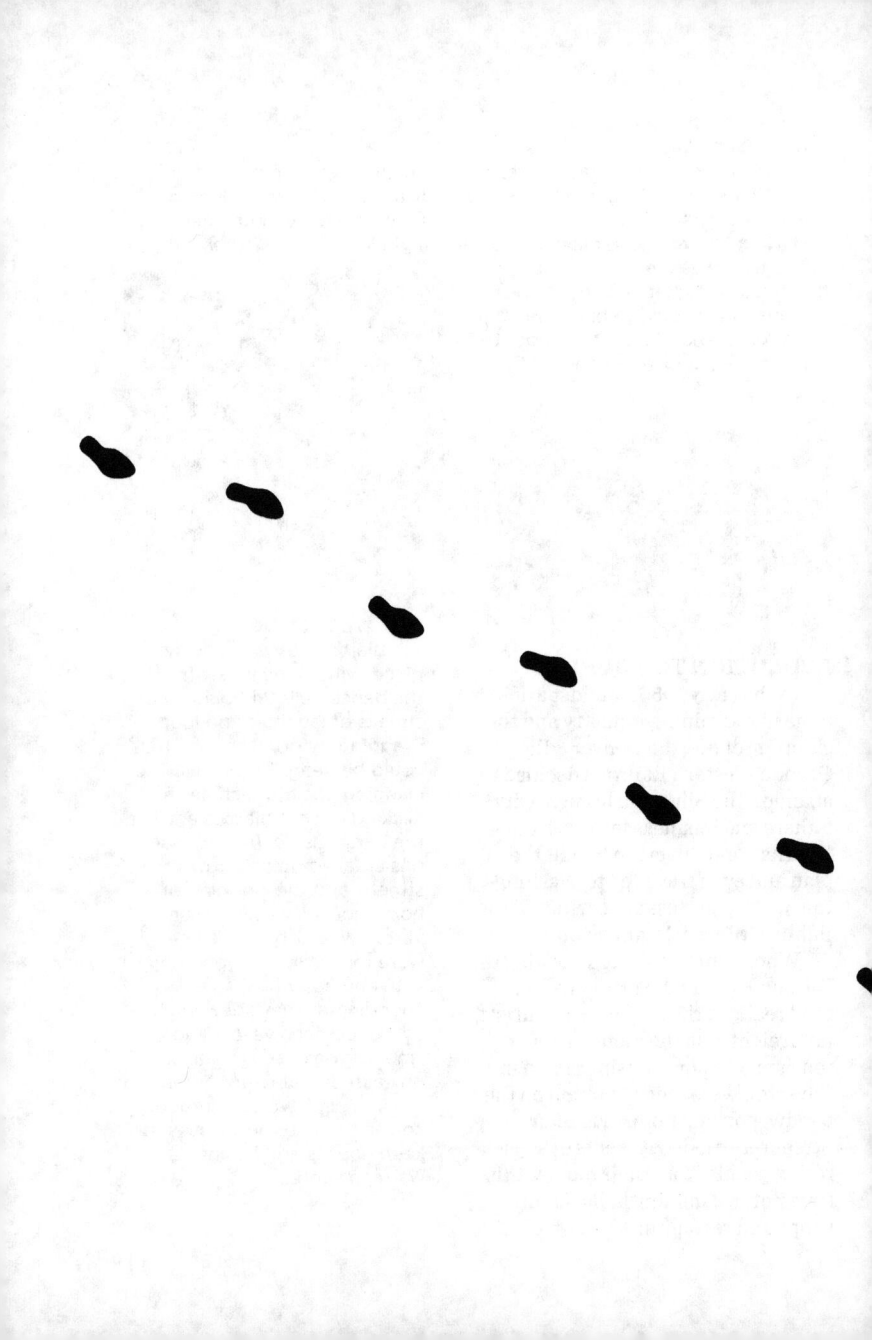

Continue on Blair Street to the intersection and look up and to your left to find this beautiful painted metal decoration.

BORDELLO

This is the oldest surviving bordello building on Blair Street, built in 1883, and known as the 557. In 1907 Battista and Ottilia Matties opened Matties Place here and purchased a $600 piano for the opulently furnished dance hall. Two years later, he added the expansion on the side. The hall was equipped with a 22-foot-long back bar with mirror, a regulation size bowling alley, a player piano, and slot machines. He also installed the ornate iron front that graces the building today. Ottilia operated a boarding house on the second floor, charging a dollar a day for room and board, including a packed lunch.

 Once an upscale den of iniquity, Natalia's is now a restaurant.

 Turn and look at the building across the street.

THE SHADY LADY

The front section of the Shady Lady Saloon was a crib operated by Kate Starr and Mamie Murphy for many years. But the best known madam was Jew Fanny, who was considered a good friend by people from all walks of life. She was Silverton's last prostitute and left town in 1949.

Next to Matties Place was the crib of **Lola Daggett and her sister Freda**. Next door to them was the Bon Ton, a bordello opened by Dottie Watson in 1899. According to a deed, she furnished it with 17 room carpets, a stair carpet, 9 three-piece bedroom sets (plus springs and mattresses), 2 sets of parlor furniture, 4 heating stoves, a large mirror – and 21 window shades.

26

Cross the street and look to your right.
There may not be any snow on Kendall Mountain behind it,
but try to find this colorful building.

 Bootleggers and billiards players used to hang out here.

THE OLD ARCADE

The **Old Arcade** is one of the newest buildings on Blair Street. Built during the depression in 1929, the Arcade Recreation Hall served bootleg whiskey and employed several sporting women in the back room. It also has been a pool hall, saloon, and gambling house. Today the building looks much the same as when it was built, including its bright orange color.

ERRAND BOYS

Many boys in Silverton made extra money by running errands for the prostitutes on Blair Street. They walked up and down the street watching the doors. If a door was closed and the red light was off, the woman had a customer. Doors were left ajar when the women needed groceries or other supplies from Greene Street, where they were not allowed. They would hand lists and money in envelopes to the boys, who went to the store and brought back the orders. The 25¢ they were paid was a fortune for the boys.

NO PAGLIACCI HERE

Silverton's first opera house, which opened in 1891, was on Blair Street. Colorado had more than 150 such theaters in the late 1800s and early 1900s. Contrary to the name, opera houses featured a wide variety of performing arts, lectures, and even sporting events.

Productions were put on by locals as well as touring artists.

Walk to nearly the end of the block.
You'll have to look up on your left to find this fancy brickwork.

WALKING SILVERTON

 The Villa Dallavalle has been owned by the same family since it was built.

VILLA DALLAVALLE

Built by John Dallavalle in 1902, this was the most substantial building on Blair Street for many years. It housed the Tyrolean saloon and a boardinghouse for many years. After John died, his wife Domenica took over the business while also operating a boarding house on Cement Creek and raising their eleven children. She and two of her sons died during the 1918 flu epidemic, leaving 16-year-old Mary, her eldest, to work and raise the family. Mary Dalla Swanson converted the building to a grocery store in the late 1940s and ran it until the 1980s.

DEATH IN THE SNOW

John Dallavalle was helping Silverton friends drive a small herd of cattle through the mountains in November 1911, when they were caught in a fierce snowstorm. For three days and with frozen feet, John pressed on, breaking trail for the others before finally reaching a cabin. One man froze to death, and ten days after having one foot amputated, John succumbed to pneumonia.

ORIGINAL TOWN HALL

Silverton built its first town hall in this block in 1883, complete with a second floor and a bell tower. It was flanked by a crib to the south, and in 1896 the Stone Saloon was built on the north side. Proper ladies who had business at the town hall didn't want to go over to Blair Street, so almost as soon as building was completed, people began calling for new town offices somewhere else in town. A new town hall was eventually built on Greene Street in 1908.

 Look at the stone building next to Villa Dallavalle.

PIEDMONTESE VS. TYROLEANS

Wars and shifting borders had fostered a rivalry between the Piedmont and Tyrol regions of northern Italy. Immigrants from those regions kept up the rivalry in Silverton. Although they all spoke some version of Italian, the Piedmontese considered the Tyroleans Austrian. The rivalry was sometimes friendly and sometimes violent, and a dividing line developed between them on Blair Street, with the Piedmontese saloons on one side and the Tyrolean saloons on the other. The Stone Saloon and Villa Dallavalle were Tyrolean, while the Bellview Saloon across the street was Piedmontese. By the early 1900s, the two groups owned almost every saloon and bordello in Silverton. In the 1950s, the Piedmontese side of the street was transformed for a movie, and the Bellview was renamed Ash's Saloon.

NEVER A GROOM

The tragic story of Peter Dalla illustrates the feud between Tyroleans and Piedmontese. Peter was 17 when he came to America. He worked hard in the mines, saved his money, and bought this building, then called the Stone Saloon.

The Italian widow of Louis Sartore, Angelina, owned the Bellview Saloon and rooming house. Peter and her daughter Katie fell in love and planned to be married in May 1904. Angelina vehemently opposed the marriage because Peter was "Austrian."

The night before the wedding, Barney Fiore, a Piedmontese who also was in love with Katie, went to the Stone Saloon and shot Peter in the thigh, shattering the bone. Peter recovered.

A week before the rescheduled wedding, as Peter slept, several sticks of dynamite exploded on the outside wall of his bedroom. He was killed, and although his murder was deemed "felonious," no one was ever charged.

Continue to the corner and turn left.
Can you find this painted floral corbel in the middle of the block?

| 69

 Standard Bottling Works sold fruit ciders and sodas as well as beer.

BOTTLING WORKS

Between 1881 and 1915, Silverton had a dozen breweries. Many of Silverton's breweries were founded by men with names like Fischer, Schultz, and Noll, immigrants from Germany, where beer brewing was an art. Not to be outdone, the Italians quickly got into the act. Along with beer, they made wine, importing grapes by the boxcar-load from the San Luis Valley.

Silverton also had several bottling operations, including the **Standard Bottling Works,** that bottled everything, including soda pop. Probably the most famous of the breweries was the Silverton Brewery. Located along the banks of Mineral Creek at the base of Sultan Mountain, it was built in 1901 by Charles Fischer. In 1919, after prohibition was enacted, the brewery fell into disrepair. But it lives on: the alcove behind the Christ of the Mines Shrine on Anvil Mountain is made of stones from the old brewery!

CHINESE EXPULSION

Prejudice against Chinese residents came to a head around Blair Street. For years, the Chinese operated laundries and restaurants in Silverton. They were referred to as heathens for their religious beliefs, and scorned for operating opium joints. Many of the women on Blair Street took to the "pipe" to relieve their dreary existence. In February 1902, a letter to the newspaper from the local union urged people to rid the town of the Chinese, saying "THEY MUST GO." A group of local men rounded up the Chinese one night, took them to the depot, and told them to walk down the tracks and not come back. They did as they were told.

Go to the intersection and turn right onto Greene Street. You'll have to stop right away and look up to your right to find this light.

 This restaurant started out as a general store.

IN A BIT OF A PICKLE

This is one of the earliest masonry buildings in Silverton, built in 1880 as a general store by Sherwin and Houghton. The newspaper reported it had 90 feet of handsome, substantial counters made of black walnut with French walnut trim, which cost more than $1,000. All of the store's furnishings were brought over Stony Pass by mules. The building served as a retail space until 1900 when it was turned into the Iron Mountain Saloon by Chiono and Giacomelli. If you look closely, you can still see the sign painted on the side of the building. After prohibition, the Giacomellis operated it as a soda fountain and confectionery store.

MODERN HONOR

The building next to the Pickle Barrel is actually new, built in the 1970s. It is a fine example of an in-fill building designed to honor the turn-of-the-century architecture of the National Historic Landmark District. There is a divide amongst historians – one side says that new construction in a historic district should be "of its

time" to differentiate it from the old, while the other side says that it should be built in the same style, so as to honor the street-scape.

FIRE

A January 1890 fire destroyed all but two buildings in this block. The original wood frame courthouse adjacent to the Sherwin and Houghton store was later dismantled, leaving the stone **Pickle Barrel building** the only surviving structure from what was once Silverton's busiest commercial block. This block alone has been damaged by more fires than the rest of the downtown combined.

There's lots to see in this block, so walk just past the Pickle Barrel and look across the street for this name.

WALKING SILVERTON

 You have found the W. C. Rogers building.

CELEBRATED PAST

W. C. Rogers built this substantial structure as a rental property in 1909. One section held a saloon, and the other a jewelry store. A disastrous fire in the early morning of July 2, 1911, almost destroyed the building. By mid-August, it was reopened as the Frog Saloon, which moved from the Teller House building. After Prohibition forced saloons out of business in 1916, the Star Theatre opened, offering live performances and that newest entertainment: movies, accompanied by a piano played at the side of the screen. The theater closed in the 1980s.

 Look for identical buildings north of the Rogers building.

TWIN BUILDINGS

Close friends William "Billy" Cole and Fritz Hoffman put their names on the cornice caps after completing these twin buildings in 1901. Cole, an Irish immigrant, and his pregnant 16-year-old wife worked as railroad construction camp cooks in 1881, when the Denver & Rio Grande was building tracks from Durango to Silverton. After the train reached Silverton, they opened a restaurant and then a boarding house here. In 1890, he started Gentlemen's Furnishings Store in a former saloon. That building was torn down to make way for this handsome edifice. Above the clothing store, Cole's son operated an alcohol-free billiards parlor. Next door, Hoffman, a German immigrant, had a first-class hardware store. Cole worked in

his store until the day he died in March 1932. Friends from Durango braved an intense winter storm to attend his funeral, having to complete the trip by toboggan because snowslides blocked the train. In April 2011, fire heavily damaged both buildings, which housed a saloon, brewery, and antique store. They have been rebuilt.

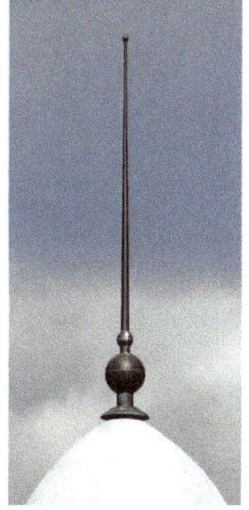

31

Keep walking north to the corner and look up to your right – way up.
Can you find this pole on top of the dome?

| 75

 Here's another building from Silverton's Glittering Decade.

CELEBRATED PAST

The **town hall**, one of three major construction projects going on in 1908, was plagued with problems. The first contractor built the basement and foundation, then died. The second contractor built the first floor, then left town. The town refused his wife's request to have his bond returned. The third contractor was fired after the front columns collapsed into the street.

Although this building and the courthouse were built at the same time, they have distinct architectural differences. With its simple four-square layout, the courthouse is quite modern. In contrast, the town hall has a much earlier design, and is quite unusual with the front door offset by the fire bay doors on one side and windows on the other.

RISING FROM THE ASHES

At the end of a long Thanksgiving holiday on Nov. 30, 1992, the town hall caught fire. The roof collapsed and the bell in the tower crashed down into the first floor. Townspeople were devastated, crying, in shock. We decided to save our town hall, and so undertook a three-year restoration project while acting as our own contractors. At the same time, the building was brought up to code, with modern electrical wiring and handicapped access. After it was done, we won a national award from the National Trust for Historic Preservation.

32

Now turn around and look across the street to find this fine stone pediment on the corner building.

PACKING IT OUT

Louis Wyman emigrated from Germany in 1871, at age 13. He worked as a cowboy in New Mexico, then came to Silverton in 1876, riding his only possession – his horse. Within a few years, he had the largest packing and freighting outfit in the county. He hauled ore and supplies for all the big mines – the Silver Lake, North Star, Polar Star, Pride of the West, and others. By 1895, he employed fifty men, and his outfit consisted of 140 pack mules, 65 burros, 5 six-horse teams, 3 four-mule teams, and a vast amount of equipment. His animals ate 15 railcars of baled hay and 4 cars of grain every month. In that same time frame, they could carry more than 1,500 tons of ore, all packed in sacks. Wyman, who served as a town trustee and county commissioner, worked tirelessly for good roads in Southwest Colorado.

 You are looking at the Wyman Building.

BETTING ON REAL ESTATE

Aerial tramways became more efficient than **pack animals**, so in 1900 Louis Wyman sold his entire freighting outfit to the British government. He took his animals and equipment to St. Louis. Everything was floated on barges to New Orleans, then taken by freighter to South Africa where they were used to transport supplies for the British Army during the Boer War. Wyman turned to developing real estate, including the Wyman Addition on the north side of Silverton. On the site of his old freighting office on Greene Street, he built the **Wyman Building**, using distinctive rose-colored sandstone, which was quarried on South Mineral Creek. He chiseled the image of the burro over the doorway as a testament to the animal that had made him wealthy.

33

Continue north on Greene Street for one block and find this decorative trim on a building to your right.

 Emergency services are based here, in the Fred Wolfe Carriage House.

VOLUNTEERS TO THE RESCUE

The carriage house honors Fred Wolfe, a volunteer fireman for many years. It houses the town's road and bridge department, emergency services office, search and rescue, and the fire department. The new fire station was built in the summer of 2014. Silverton depends on volunteers. Virtually everyone in town volunteers, whether it is on government boards like the planning commission, avalanche board, or downtown improvement association, or as EMTs or firemen. This town could not run without its volunteers.

SPARED FROM FIRE

Unlike many mining towns throughout the West, Silverton had only one major fire. Except for the 1890 fire, which destroyed most of the 1300 block of Greene Street on the east side, fires were contained to individual structures. Early mining towns were susceptible to fires because they were heated with wood or coal and built mostly of connected wood frame buildings. Those towns that survived the destruction of their business districts by fire enacted regulations requiring fire-resistant building materials like brick and stone.

Most of Silverton's first generation of wooden buildings didn't burn, but were torn down to make way for more substantial brick and stone buildings, demonstrating the wealth of the burgeoning town.

34

As you continue to the corner and cross the street, look for a monument with this small copper plaque.

 Don't miss the map on top of this monument to mining.

MINING MONUMENT

This monument pays tribute to the area's complex geology and rich mining history. Volcanoes, glaciers, and inland seas have all played a part in shaping the San Juan Mountains, but volcanic action is what formed the precious metals that prospectors and miners have sought for 150 years. As super-heated water rose through cracks, it cooled and deposited the minerals in hardrock veins. Those faults and veins are where the gold, silver, lead, copper, and zinc are found. Look on top of the monument for a map of where all the mines were located.

MINING TO SKIING

Mining in the San Juans helped give rise to the skiing industry. The gondolas that carry skiers up the slopes grew out of technology that was developed here. Because of the volcanic formation of the San Juans, the ore tended to be at high altitude. **Trams** were created to carry the ore in iron buckets down from the mines to the mills far below. This technology allowed mines to work year-round because the trams carried ore high above the snow, so access roads didn't have to be plowed.

DIE HARD SPORTSMEN

Winter offers its own opportunities here, with skiing, ice skating, and sledding at Kendall Mountain Recreation Area, a town-operated area that caters to families. Silverton Mountain – the nation's only new ski area in thirty years – is for "extreme" expert skiers and is ranked #1 in the U.S. for steeps and powder. Cross country skiing takes people into some of the most unspoiled landscapes in the world and snowmobiling brings folks from all over the state to enjoy snow conditions that rival the best anywhere. Silvertonians even golf in the winter, on a groomed nine-hole, par 3 course with painted holes and colored balls.

35

Continue to the parking lot where you started the tour and look for this sign.

 The sign you have found is on the museum.

FROM JAIL TO MUSEUM

The three-story brick and cut sandstone Italianate building in front of you was Silverton's third jail, built after prisoners escaped from earlier log prisons. Almost all the building's historic features remain intact, including decorative belt courses, segmental arched window headers, stone foundation, and porches with decorative balustrades, spindles, and gabled stoops. The original tool-proof cells and related hardware were custom-made at a St. Louis, Missouri, foundry.

The first prisoner, 38-year-old Andy Johnson, was incarcerated for nearly six months for burglary. The jailer's wife prepared all his meals in the residential quarters on the first floor.

The building was a home for elderly, indigent miners in the 1930s. After World War II, it sat vacant until the **San Juan County Historical Society** developed it as a museum.

PAYING TRIBUTE

From the courthouse parking lot, you can look toward the north and see **Hillside Cemetery** on the lower flanks of Boulder Mountain. It is rocky ground, steep in places. There are no manicured paths or gardens, although nature adorns it with trees and wildflowers. The first known burial there was in 1875. Markers for many of the early graves have disappeared over time. In October and November 1918, more than half the town became ill in the Spanish influenza epidemic. Undertakers ran out of coffins and graves couldn't be dug fast enough to keep up with the fatalities. Two trenches were dug in the cemetery for many of the 150 people who died.

WALKING SILVERTON

Great Finish!

You are now back to where you started the tour. We hope you have enjoyed learning about Silverton and the people who have called it home over the past century and a half. Perhaps you can envision those early prospectors hacking away at the mountains in search of gold, the first merchants building and stocking their stores, or the packers whose mules and burros kept goods and ore moving in the high mountains.

Whether you prefer Quality Hill or nortorious Blair Street, we hope you'll want to learn more about Silverton. Here are some places where you will find stories and photos from our past:

>Jail Museum and Mining Heritage Center
>Hillside Cemetery
>Mayflower Mill
>Old Hundred Mine Tour
>Animas Forks
>Durango & Silverton depot
>Many local businesses

To learn about other things to see and do in Silverton, visit:

>Visitor Information Center, 414 Greene Street
>San Juan National Forest Field Station, 1468 Greene Street
>   (May 15-Sept. 15)
>www.silvertoncolorado.com
>www.sanjuancountyhistoricalsociety.org

TO LEARN MORE

Many More Mountains, volumes 1, 2, & 3, by Allen Nossaman

The Story of Hillside Cemetery, volumes 1 & 2, by Freda Carley Peterson

Salone Italiano, by Kay Niemann

Bordellos of Blair Street, by Allan G. Bird

Silverton Then & Now, by Allan G. Bird

Exploring the Historic San Juan Triangle, by P. David Smith

Ghosts and Gold, by Scott Fetchenhier

A Brief History of Silverton, by Duane A. Smith

Mining the Hard Rock, by Zeke Zanoni & John Marshall

My Home at Present, by Mark A. Vendle, Duane A. Smith, & Karen A. Vendle

Animas Forks, by Will Meyerriecks

ACKNOWLEDGMENTS

Without the years of dedicated research by Allen Nossaman, Allan Bird, and Freda Carley Peterson, this book would not have been possible. Allen's three-volume *Many More Mountains* and Freda's *Story of Hillside Cemetery* are the kind of detailed histories that most historical societies can only dream about having. Allan Bird's meticulously researched *Bordellos of Blair Street* helped immensely with that part of town.

We also thank Ray Dileo for his photographs and Marybelle Beigh, Melanie Bergole, Mark Esper, Gay Kiene, Rich Robinson, Penny Salka, Lisa Stockebrand, Pete Varney, Robert & Nancy Whitson, and Judy Zimmerman for helping to fine-tune the tour. Thanks to Lisa Whittington for letting us copy an old photo of John Dallavalle and Patty Dailey for being so hospitable at the Brown Bear Café.

We also appreciate the Durango Herald Small Press for providing San Juan County Historical Society the impetus and guidance to produce this book. And we thank Elizabeth Green for being a wonderful editor who kept us on track and on schedule with good humor and lots of praise. It has been a pleasure to work with her.

Beverly Rich was born and raised in Silverton, and attended Silverton High School and Fort Lewis College. Her father and her late husband Bill were both miners. She resides in a Victorian-era house, loves the mountains, and was the San Juan County Treasurer for 24 years. As chairman of the San Juan County Historical Society, she has raised more than $10 million in grants for historic preservation projects in Silverton and San Juan County. So it's not surprising that the National Trust for Historic Preservation gave her a National Honor Award for her work in preserving history.

PHOTO CREDITS

Present-day photographs are by Casey Carroll unless otherwise noted:

Ray Dileo: clue photos on pgs. 39, 41, 45, 49, 51, 53, 61, 71, 73, 79; p. 14, house; p. 16, Boulder Mountain; p. 22, school entrance; p. 34, shrine; p. 48, tower house; p. 72, Pickle Barrel; p. 82, mine monument.

Stephen F. Rich: gunfighters, pg. 59.

All historic photos are the property of San Juan County Historical Society unless otherwise noted:

Lisa Whittington, pg. 66, John Dallavalle.

INDEX

Architecture
    Gingerbread 12, 25, 26, 34
    Italianate 20, 84
    Mining camp vernacular style 56
    Pre-WWI architecture 48
    Queen Anne style 12, 34
    Shotgun houses 56
Baker, Charles 20
Baker's Park 5, 56
Banks
    Bank of Silverton 40
    First National Bank of Silverton 40
    Miners and Merchants Bank of Lake City 40
    San Juan County Bank 40
    Silverton Industrial Bank 40
Benson Block 44
Benson, Knute 44
Billiards parlor 40, 74
Black population 32
Blair, Thomas 38, 56
Blockade, 1932 9
Boarding houses 5, 54, 62, 74
    Alma House 52
    Villa Dallavalle 66, 67
Boer War 78
Bordello 58, 67
    557 62
    Bon Ton 62
Bowling alley 40, 62
Bowman, Clint 46
Breweries 70
Brothels 56, 58
Carnegie libraries 28, 40
Carnegie, Andrew 28
Charles Fischer 42
Chicago World's Fair 16
Chief Ouray 24
Chinese 32, 38, 70
Christ of the Mines Shrine 34, 70
Christmas dinner 22
Churches
    African Methodist Episcopal 32
    Catholic Men's Club 34
    Foursquare Church 24
    Silverton Congregational Church 29
    St. John's Episcopal Church 24
    St. Patrick's Catholic Church 32
    Southern Baptist 24
Civil War 20, 24, 54
Cole, William "Billy" 74
Corbel 37
Cotton, Amanda 16
Cotton, John 16
County Assessor 9
Courthouse 40
Cribs 58, 62, 66
Cross country skiing 82
Curry, John R. 18
Daggett, Freda 62
Daggett, Lola 62
Dairies 36
Dalla, Peter 67
Dallavalle, Domenica 66
Dallavalle, John 66
Dance halls 56, 59, 62
    Matties Place 62
Doud brothers 42
Earl, William 14
Earp, Wyatt 56
Edbrooke, F.E. 20
Eureka 24
Expeditionary Learning 22
F. O. Sherwood 26
Fanny, Jew 62
Fattor, Big Tillie 58
Fiore, Barney 67
Fire 18, 54, 58, 72, 74, 76, 80
    Fire department 12
Fischer, Charles 70
Fish farm 36
Flu epidemic of 1918 66, 84
Fourth of July parade 50
Fraternal organizations
    Eagles 18
    Elks, 18
    Knights of Pythias 18
    Masonic Lodge 18
    Odd Fellows 18
    Silverton Men's Club 18
    Woodsmen of the World 18, 36
Fred Wolfe Carriage House 80
French Bakery 42
Gable, Clark 59
Gambling 38, 50, 56, 59, 64
Gentlemen's Furnishings Store 74
Glittering Decade 40, 50, 76

Golf 82
Greene & Co. mercantile 14
Greene Smelter 12, 14, 36
Greene, George 36
Grivette, Joe 44
Gunfights 58
HARDROCK 100 22, 54
Hardrockers' Holidays 44
Harris, Emma 26, 34
Harwood, Ben 14
Hemboldt, Fred 36
Hillside Cemetery 26, 84
Hoffman, Fritz 74
Hotels
    Avon Hotel 54
    Grand Hotel 8, 38
    Grand Imperial Hotel 38, 44
    Teller House 42, 74
Howardsville 58
Hudson, Amelia 29
Hudson, Marvin 29
Hudson, Pauline 29
Hughes, Bridget 52
Hughes, John 52
Hughes, May 52
Johnson, Andy 84
Jones, Casey 52
Kendall Mountain Recreation Area 82
Kendall, James W. 16
Kendrick-Gelder Smelter 12
Kimball, Alice Hendrickson 9
Lake City 22
Lake Emma 34
Liveries
    Bowman and Melton livery stable 46
    Exchange Livery 42
    Patterson Bros. Livery 46
Lorenzen, John 44
Lynchings 42
Masterson, Bat 56
Matties, Battista 62
Matties, Ottilia 62
Mears, Otto 24, 32, 52
Merchants Biscuit Company 46
Miners' Union
    Founding 20
    Hall 48
    Miners' Union Hospital 20, 40
    Strike 48
Mines 40
    American Tunnel 34
    Gold King 5, 46
    Highland Mary 14
    Mayflower 48
    North Star 78
    Old Hundred 5
    Pride of the West 78
    Red Mountain Mining District 12
    Silver Lake 78
    Sunnyside Mine 5, 34
Mining 5, 12, 20, 54, 59, 82
    Base metals 54
    Mining Monument 82
    Safety 20
    Terms 44
Monroe, Marilyn 59
Mountains
    Anvil Mountain 16, 34
    Boulder Mountain 12, 16, 84
    Geology 82
    Grand Turk 16
    Handies Peak 22
    Kendall Mountain 14, 16, 63
    Sultan Mountain 16
    Stony Pass 5, 14, 72
    Storm Peak 16
Movies 56, 59
    Across the Wide Missouri 56
    Maverick Queen 56
    Run for Cover 56
    Ticket to Tomahawk 59
    True Grit 56
Municipal light plant 46
Murphy, Mamie 62
Museum 84
National Historic Landmark District 4, 8, 72
National Historic Site in Journalism 18
Newspapers
    La Plata Miner 18
    Silverton Standard 18, 50
    Silverton Standard and Miner 18
Ogsbury, Clayt 42
Old Town Square 58
Opera house 64
Opium dens 70
Ouray 22, 29
Outlaws 42
Packing
    Pack animals 77, 78
    Pack trains 40, 52, 78

Packer 24
Pascoe Opera House 50
Pascoe, J.N., Dr. 50
Pickle Barrel 72
Piedmont vs. Tyrol 67
Posey & Wingate building 40
Prosser undertaking 48
Quality Hill 26
Railroads 24, 36, 40, 54, 59
    Depot 52
    Denver & Rio Grande Railroad 5, 52, 74
    Denver & Rio Grande Western Railroad 59
    Durango & Silverton tracks 59
    Railroad passes 32
    Silverton Gladstone and Northerly Railroad 12
Reese, Dempsey 12
Rogers, W.C. 74
Russian princess 34
Saloons 44, 50, 56, 67
    Bellview Saloon 67
    Bent Elbow 58
    Chicago Saloon 44
    Diamond Saloon 42
    Fattor Saloon 58
    Iron Mountain Saloon 72
    Monte Carlo Saloon 58
    Old Arcade 64
    Polar Star 78
    Rosebud Saloon 56
    San Juan Bar 36
    Shady Lady Saloon 62
    Stone Saloon 66, 67
    The Club 38
    The Frog 42, 74
    The Tyrol 42
    Tyrolean saloon 66
    Zanoni-Pedroni Saloon 58
San Juan County Courthouse 8
San Juan County Historical Society 84
San Juan County Jail 8, 40, 84
Sartore, Angelina 67
Sartore, Katie 67
Sherwin and Houghton store 72
Sherwood & Son's Grocery 54
Silver panic, 1893 48
Silverton Brass Band 50
Silverton Brewery 42, 70
Silverton Library 28

Silverton Meat and Produce 36
Silverton Mountain 82
Silverton School 22
Skiing 82
Smelters 36, 40, 52, 59
Snowslides 9, 18, 20
    East Riverside Slide 29
Snowden, Francis M. 20, 26
Snowmobiling 82
Standard Bottling Works 70
Star Theatre 74
Starr, Kate 62
Stewart, Jimmy 59
Streets 3, 36
    10th Street 52
    Blair Street 56
    Empire Street 56
    Greene Street 36
    Reese Street 12
    Snowden Street 26
Swanson, Mary Dalla 66
Taft, Anna Silverton 14
Taft, Byron 14
Taft, Sarah 14
Telluride 22
Thanksgiving dinner 22
Thompson, W.S. 38
Tourism 59
Tower house 48
Town Hall 40, 66, 76
Trams 5, 12, 54, 78, 82
Utes 5
Volunteers 80
Wagons 52, 59, 80
    Wagon road 5
Watson, Dottie 62
Wayne, John 59
Western Rocky Mountain Brass Band Festival 50
Whitelaw, Harold "Kid" 44
Wingate, J. W. 34, 40
Wolfe, Fred 80
Works Progress Administration 22
World War II 54
Wyman Building 78
Wyman, Louis 78

www.ingramcontent.com/pod-product-compliance
Lightning Source LLC
LaVergne TN
LVHW021952060526
838201LV00049B/1684